LITTLE BOOK OF
MEERKATS

Michelle Brachet

LITTLE BOOK OF

MEERKATS

First published in the UK in 2012

© Demand Media Limited 2012

www.demand-media.co.uk

Printed and bound in China

ISBN 978-1-909217-15-7

CONTENTS

INTRODUCTION

Known as the 'Sun Angel' in certain parts of Africa due to its supposed protective powers against the 'Moon Devil', which was believed to attack lone tribesmen or stray animals, the meerkat took its name from an Afrikaans (Dutch population in South Africa) word and was first named in 1776. Meaning 'marsh-cat' in English, although it doesn't live near marshes, nor is it a cat, the meerkat is a small mammal that belongs to the mongoose family.

In general, meerkats have fairly dark markings on their bodies and have bands around the eyes that make them look like they're wearing sunglasses. This band is protective and helps to reflect the glare of the sun so that meerkats can see clearly in the hot environment in which they live. Each

foot has four toes with non-retractable claws, but they can close their ears. An adult can reach up to 12 inches in height and weighs, on average, around two pounds. Their tails grow up to eight inches long and are used as a tripod to balance the mammal when they are in an upright position. These creatures are diurnal, which means that they are active during the day and sleep at night.

Meerkats communicate effectively between themselves by using sounds, scent and body language. There are more than 20 sounds in the meerkat vocabulary and each particular noise has a distinct meaning. There are alarm calls, which indicate both the danger of predators and of approaching weather systems. There are also lost calls, leading calls, feeding calls, foraging calls and sentry calls. Foraging calls, for example,

help those out looking for food to keep track of the others' locations and teach young pups learning to forage how to remain within earshot of the family. There are also a number of different calls for playing or wrestling, play-fighting and grooming.

Meerkats are the first non-human mammals to be seen actively teaching their young. Although some characteristics of their behaviour are instinctive, others are not. For example, a meerkat bred outside the natural environment which then becomes pregnant will not know how to teach her own pups to survive. Within the meerkat group this is done by 'mentors', or elders who show the young pup how to eat a venomous scorpion, for example. Altruistic behaviour, however, doesn't always shine through and meerkats have been known to kill the young of the alpha male and alpha female in order to advance their own offspring's chances of survival, or to propel themselves up the ladder of hierarchy within the group as a whole.

New meerkat groups will appear and threaten dominant, established tribes when females that have been evicted from the original group set themselves up with male meerkats from rival groups who are looking to mate. In situations where a group becomes too large to sustain itself, then it is common for certain members of the group to disperse and find alternative meerkat groups, which can support them in terms of food resources, for example.

With a life span of 12 to 14 years, one particularly interesting fact about meerkats is that they have the ability to absorb heat from the sun. Often described as the 'solar panel of the animal world', meerkats use their bellies – with its sparse fur – to warm up during daylight hours.

CHAPTER 1

FAMILY DYNAMICS

Meerkats are fairly monogamous mammals and will try to mate for life. Mating usually takes place between the alpha male and the alpha female, but should the dominant male die or be killed by a predator, then other males will show their own dominance in order to become the new top male.

Other reasons that mating may take place without the alpha male's involvement include, a rival gang member ousting the dominant male, or females mating with a member of a rival family. This would take place whilst out foraging for food and is done without the knowledge of the alpha male. The dominant female will chase all female family members away (those 10 months or older) when she is ready to mate. This can result in lesser females mating with males from other groups and sometimes joining a rival group. If the lesser female becomes impregnated she will often abort the pups. If not, she may try to sneak her own offspring into the breeding burrow and put them with those of the dominant female. However, if the alpha female realises that not all the pups are her own, she will kill and eat the intruding pups.

The alpha female chases beta females away until after giving birth so that her pups are the only ones belonging to the group or mob, however, once her strength has returned, the lesser females are allowed to return to the burrow and will be allowed to help feed milk to the newborn pups. Meerkats are able to breed every two or three months, but successful breeding two or three times a year is more likely due to food resources.

Gestation lasts 70 days and litters consist of five or six newborn pups. These tiny pups are born with their eyes closed and they stay in the breeding den for the first two weeks of their life where they suckle milk from their mother and other females who are lactating.

At this time, they are completely help-less and one job in the meerkat mob is babysitting. Between two and three weeks following birth, the new pups are encouraged outside the burrow and are left close to the entrance for protection with babysitters. Often, these babysitters will endanger their own lives in order to protect the offspring of the alpha female. If possible, they will take the young underground should a danger present itself and, will stand and face the predator or danger should it follow the young into the burrow. However, if no bolthole or burrow is within easy distance then the babysitter will huddle the young together and lie on top of them in order to protect them from any impending danger.

The alpha female will need to eat in order to keep up her milk supply for the pups and so the other members of the mob look after the youngsters. During this time the alpha female is not required to watch her young and is given less duties so that she can concentrate on enabling her pups to gain strength. By about six weeks the pups are ready to forage with the other meerkats while their diet is supple-mented with milk. At four months old the pups are ready to forage for their own food. Older members of the mob take responsibility for one pup and act as a type of mentor during their formative months by showing them how to develop their life skills and, most importantly of all, how to survive.

At 11 months a meerkat reaches matu-rity and is then able to venture out of the burrow on its own. Some may join other mobs or form gangs of their own. Others may look for breeding opportunities among rival mobs, but some young meerkats opt to stay with their own mob for two or three years. It is also usual for young adults to leave the gang in small groups.

The alpha male and female have the most breeding rights and are obviously the dominant members of the mob. The beta male is a young meerkat of 10 to 11 months or older who hasn't yet left the mob. Beta females support the alpha female until they are ready to leave the mob in search of their own breeding opportunities. Meerkats aged six months or older are often given babysitting duties, while sentries are made up of male and female members of the mob who are responsible for watching over the gang and for alerting their group to any possible or imminent dangers. Other meerkats are responsible for digging burrows, which they tend to do in gangs in order to be more efficient and save time.

CHAPTER 2

GANG **CULTURE**

Meerkats rely on living in groups to survive. With around 30 to 40 or so meerkats in the group, most are the siblings or offspring of the alpha pair. It is usual for the alpha male and alpha female to scent the subordinates in the group, as much of meerkat recognition is achieved by marking rather than by sight.

Known as 'mobs', 'gangs' or 'clans', these colonial animals are extremely sociable within their own groups. Subordinates to the alpha male and female are known to groom the bodies and lick the faces of the dominant pair to show loyalty and recognition. They are willing to share food, snuggle and lick each other for affection, and will groom other members before settling down to sleep in a huge haphazard pile; a bit like puppies in a litter would do.

This represents an incredibly close-knit mob and helps to keep them warm (as meerkats are particularly sensitive to the cold). This is not only a night-time display of camaraderie; they also show their desire for closeness during daylight hours.

The day will see meerkats foraging for food on the open savannah. As this is dangerous for these small mammals, one 'sentry' or guard, along with others in the group, takes a turn at keeping watch by standing on its hind legs as it scours the skies for predators. The meerkat 'on duty' will keep a vigilant eye on the sky, an action that conveys to the others that the area is safe. Sometimes a guard will perch in the branches of trees or bushes to ensure that the 'family' is safe from the dangers of predators.

means that workers are extremely hungry when their duties are finished. Food is found by pawing and sniffing at the ground. Once food is evident the meerkats commence a digging frenzy in order to obtain the prey. As many of the meerkats' prey are fairly fast moving, these animals have adapted themselves so that they can shift their own bodyweight in sand in a matter of minutes.

The non-retractable claws on their paws and hind legs also enable the meerkats to dig burrows, which comprise extensive passages underground. Burrows are essential for escaping predators as well as the hot sun, and for sleeping and raising young. Play fighting is a pastime for pups, young meerkats and older members of the mob alike as it helps to teach social structure and dominance within the gang. Scientists and experts also advocate that where conditions in the Kalahari are intensely harsh, it has been crucial that meerkats develop a form of bonding that leads to helping rear each other's young in order to survive.

A mob gives the meerkat greater strength in numbers, as being fairly small they need to pool resources. This means that there is a 'division of labour' with certain meerkats taking responsibility for different jobs. Some of these jobs include babysitting pups, sharing, taking guard duty and foraging for food.

Each and every meerkat is at some point given leave to eat, which means that another willing worker immediately takes their place. As a warmblooded mammal with a relatively high metabolism (environment allowing), meerkats need to eat every few minutes. This

CHAPTER 3

HABITAT

The majority of meerkats in the world live in the area known as the Kalahari Desert in Southern Africa. This vast desert spreads across South Africa, Namibia, Angola, Botswana and Zimbabwe. The open, arid savannah sees little rainfall on an annual basis. Covering more than one million square miles, the Kalahari is roughly 10 times the size of the United Kingdom and is made up of largely bright orange soft sand or porous landscape.

The Kalahari is fraught with dangers for these creatures and survival is difficult in the somewhat harsh conditions. Meerkats have, however, evolved to adapt to this desert environment. Interestingly, animals in the Kalahari have a lower metabolic rate than their counterparts in other regions of the world, which allows them to survive with less food and water – a prerequisite for life in this harsh, barren place. The intensity of the sun in the Kalahari, however, puts all animals in danger of overheating, so meerkats have the ability to regulate their body temperature, which is a necessity rather than a luxury.

Sand in the Kalahari consists of two types, soft and compact, which gives two distinct colours of landscape: white and orange. The soft sand is a favourite for the meerkats who use less energy to forage for food among the grains. However, they prefer the compact sand for building burrows. This tougher sand gives a more stable shelter, whereas burrows in soft sand would be liable to collapse.

At around 40ºC (115°F) from October

to April each year, the climate is particularly dry and hot. This can mean sand temperatures of around 70ºC (158°F). Even the shade offers little respite. Winter months are somewhat cooler, but even then the daytime heat can reach highs of 22ºC (70°F), but nights tend to be fairly cold at around -10ºC (14°F) and meerkats are long in their burrows by then.

The dry season coincides with the winter months from May to September, while the average annual rainfall (which occurs towards the end of the summer months between January and April) is around 12 inches. Naturally, this gives little surface water, however, the sand underneath does retain a fair amount of moisture. It is unusual for it to rain in the summer, but if precipitation does occur, then lush plants, flowers and other grasses join the grasses and scrubs that thinly cover the landscape.

Meerkats live in burrows under the sand. These burrows consist of numerous entrances, which also act as escape routes in times of need, as well as sleeping chambers and connecting tunnels. These entrances give easy escape routes to the safety of the earth should danger be present on the outside of the burrow. Boltholes are common in the complex burrow system as these provide cover if predators are lurking in the vicinity when the meerkats are out searching for food.

Mobs usually have a living area of between one and three square miles and they are extremely territorial. The land (and burrows underground) that the meerkats dominate is sized according to how much food and water the particular mob has access to in their territory, as well as how big the group actually is. The large mounds of sand and dirt outside the entrance to the burrow serve as a lookout for the meerkats so that they have a better view over the surrounding area for predators. Like many other animals, territory is marked using saliva or the anal gland.

The alpha male (most dominant) is responsible for territorial marking and meerkats are renowned for guarding their territory aggressively. They will stop at nothing to discourage, frighten off and defend their home from other mobs or gangs. Each mob has a number of dens, which they move every two days or so to disorientate their foes and protect their family. The only exception to this rule is the breeding den where the pups are born. Female meerkats will remain in the breeding burrow for up to three weeks from where they take the newborn pups out to learn to forage for food. If breeding in a particular season has been successful, however, then the burrow is likely to be used again in the future.

Breeding burrows are easily more identifiable than entrances to other burrows purely because there is more constant digging required in order to cope with the prolonged stay; mounds of sand may reach up to three feet high at the opening. Once the breeding den is no longer required it becomes a haven for other animals, including ground squirrels, yellow mongoose and snakes. The meerkats' faeces left behind provide food for other species such as beetles.

BUSHMEN IN THE KALAHARI DESERT

CHAPTER 4

DIET AND **SUSTENANCE**

Despite a sting that can paralyze an adult and kill a child, the scorpion is part of the meerkats' diet. These mammals have adapted over time, as have all mongoose-related family members, to become immune to the venom in the scorpion's tail and they eat them as part of a varied diet. They also eat tubers, roots, fruits and

nuts, small mammals and reptiles, including snakes, worms, crickets, spiders, beetles, centipedes and millipedes. Although meerkats do make use of water supplies when there are any, they have developed so that they gain all the liquid they need from their diet.

Insects and other creatures burrow deeper into the sand during the warmer months making foraging much harder work for the meerkats. Rain means easier foraging as the large amounts of moisture in the sand bring food sources to the surface.

Scorpions

As an arthropod, the scorpion has eight legs and belongs to the order Scorpiones, a class that also includes spiders, mites and ticks. There are around 2,000 species of scorpions across the globe and each has its body divided into two segments consisting of the prosoma and abdomen (or opisthosoma). The scorpion's tail comprises six parts, the last of which consists of the anus and sting (or telson). This holds venom glands and the barb, which is used to inject the poison. The venom itself is usually neurotoxic and is used to paralyse prey so that the scorpion can eat it. However, the venom is also used to ward off its own predators, although this doesn't work with meerkats.

If a scorpion stings a human, it will most likely cause pain, numbness and swelling. There are some scorpions that can be extremely dangerous to man, however, for example the "deathstalker" (Leiurus quinquestriatus), Androctonus, Centruroides, Parabuthus and Tityus.

The scorpion most responsible for death in humans is the yellow fat-tailed scorpion (Androctonum australis) of North Africa. This is, however, as a result of this scorpion being more common than others, rather than because its venom is more toxic. Death is likely to occur in the young, elderly or infirm rather than a healthy adult, but an allergic reaction to the venom may also result in a fatality. Venom is regulated and each sting contains between

0.1 and 0.6 milligrams of poison. It has also been noted that scorpions will only use their venom on large prey or a prey that struggles.

Scorpions have two types of venom. One is designed to stun the victim and is known to be weaker, while the other potent venom has the ability to kill a larger prey. Replenishing supplies of venom may take the scorpion up to several days, so it knows to regulate how much and what strength it injects into its victim.

Most scorpions reproduce sexually, however, some species do not and actually use parthenogenesis whereby the

unfertilised eggs can develop into living embryos. Like more evolved shark species, most scorpions are viviparous, meaning that the young are born one by one. The young scorpions are then carried on their mother's back until they have undergone at least one moult. The mother is also responsible for maintaining her offspring's moisture levels and she may have between two and 100 or so young to support during this time. Scorpions have around five or seven moults before they are considered to have reached maturity. The scorpion is at its most vulnerable when it has just undergone a moult, as the exoskeleton is soft. Stretching its body is the fastest way to ensure that its 'shell' hardens. There is little known about the lifespan of a scorpion but estimates range between four and 20 years. Unlike meerkats who like to feed on them, scorpions are nocturnal and find shelter during the hottest daytime temperatures. They burrow into the relative cool of holes and rocks during the day where they avoid their natural predators (along with meerkats) of birds, lizards, mice, rats and centipedes.

When a scorpion is attacked by a meerkat, it will automatically try to inject its neurotoxic venom in an attempt to kill or paralyse it. When this fails, the scorpion becomes lunch and the meerkat is sated for a relatively short time. The meerkat kills the scorpion by quickly biting off its tail (and stinger) before eating the remainder of its body. In the Kalahari and Botswana where the environment is harsh, scorpions survive by aestivating at times of drought.

Beetles

Meerkats also feed on many different types of bugs, and beetles are a firm favourite. These insects are easy for the mammals to obtain and are usually plentiful, as beetles constitute the majority of species of insects. Nearly 40% of all insect species are types of beetle and around 350,000 species have been identified, however, the estimated numbers of species, as yet unconfirmed, could be in the region of between five and eight million.

Beetles are able to adapt to their environment in a variety of ways and happily thrive in different ecosystems. Like other insects they both prey on other invertebrates and feed on organic matter, but they are also prey themselves for different types of birds and mammals. Beetles and their larvae (which are also attractive to meerkats) have developed a number of strategies as a defence

weevils have also developed so that they have coloured scales (or hairs), which give them the ability to resemble bird dung. Mimicry occurs in beetles that resemble other creatures, for example, some look like wasps, which fools predators into thinking that the beetle is a threat rather than a tasty meal. Mimicry, in some beetle species can even typify the behaviour of the insect or creature that it is trying to resemble. Others produce toxins, which usually go hand in hand with colour patterns and are designed to dissuade predators from eating them. Larger beetles also have the ability to 'go on the attack' in their efforts to persuade potential predators to go in search of an easier target.

from attacks by predators or parasites. This can include mimicry, toxins and camouflage, which might mean the use of colours or shapes to enable them to blend into the surrounding environment.

Leaf beetles are particularly adept at this form of defence and have a similar green colouring to their habitat. Some

Beetles are fairly uniform in their general body shape and have similar organs and limbs across species although, naturally, these can vary a fair amount in appearance. A beetle's body is divided into three sections consisting of the head, abdomen and thorax. The exoskeleton is usually hard and made up of numerous plates, which helps with its armoured defence, whilst also allowing the insect a large amount of flexibility. Ground beetles have lost the ability to fly as have weevils, and some have evolved into desert and cave-dwelling species. These beetles tend to have a shield over the abdomen.

Smell is the beetle's greatest asset and despite its huge eyes, it is able to glean a clearer idea of its environment from this function rather than from sight. Legs are mainly used for walking, but in some species limbs have been adapted for other uses too – including swimming, digging and in some cases, jumping. Beetles do not have blood, but have an open circulatory system, which is powered by a tube-like heart contained within the thorax instead.

Female beetles may lay up to several thousand eggs in a lifetime and the larvae are considered the principal feeding stage in its life cycle. Larvae feed frantically once the eggs have hatched and are easily identified by their chewing mouths. Each larva goes through several moults (or developmental stages)

before it reaches the pupate stage where a fully formed, mature adult emerges. Depending on the species, beetles have varied life spans ranging from a few weeks to several years.

Crickets

Whereas a scorpion will remain still or run from danger, crickets on the other hand advertise their whereabouts with a distinct call, or chirp, (although only males can do this). The temperature of the environment determines the rate of the chirp. The sound is produced by the

male using his wings over his ridges or 'teeth' of which there are between 50 and 300. The forewing consists of a rib or modified vein, which is raised to a 45 degree angle and then rubbed against the hind edge of the opposite forewing. This works from left to right. There are two types of call: one is used in courtship for attracting a female, while the other is designed to ward off rival males. They feed on decaying plant materials and seedlings. There are around 900 species of crickets, and meerkats like to dine out on the African field cricket (Gryllus bimaculatus) in particular.

Centipedes and Millipedes

Centipedes and millipedes are invertebrates with long segmented bodies with either one pair (centipedes) or two pairs (millipedes) of legs on each segment. Like the scorpion, centipedes use poison to paralyse their prey, which usually consists of small insects. Their poison claws are positioned behind the head, but their jaws are weak and unable to penetrate a predator. Bites that do penetrate can cause pain (similar to a bee sting) and some swelling in the affected area. Centipedes like to hide under stones, rocks or beneath moist leaves and other organic material. If disturbed, they move quickly to a predetermined hiding place and they generally require moist habitats. Millipedes are very similar to centipedes and are brown or blackish in

colour. They do not, however, have poison claws and their long body is usually rounded rather than flat. Instead of running from danger as a centipede would, millipedes tend to coil up when under threat. Millipedes also like moist places and feed on organic matter. Meerkats will drag a millipede or centipede across the sand to remove its chemical defences before eating it.

CHAPTER 5

THE **ENEMY**

When standing, meerkats can reach up to 12 inches, which means that they have a good vantage point across the surrounding terrain. They can even maintain this stance from branches of trees, which better serves them for keeping 'look-out' for danger. Their honed guarding instincts, however, do not always save them from their known predators and the harsh realities that life brings.

As highly social animals, meerkats like to play and wrestle and they wake early to take advantage of the cooler hours before the sun becomes too intense. One meerkat acts as sentry and is the first to come out of the burrow surveying the surrounding area before allowing the others access to the outside. The morning is spent foraging for food and keeping a look out for danger. When the sun is at its hottest the mob will rest before taking advantage of the cooler hours later in the day when the hunt for food resumes. Meerkats are well aware of the predators and dangers they face.

Martial Eagle

Meerkats are hunted and preyed on by the Martial eagle, a species that is seriously under threat in parts of Africa. It is, however, meerkats that face danger from this strong and relentless predator. Although the Martial eagle is widespread throughout South Africa it is in fact fairly uncommon in Botswana and the Kalahari region. Nevertheless, it is a real and serious threat. The bird is most prolific in the Kruger National Park and the Kgalagadi Park in South Africa, as well as the Chobe National Park. In

Namibia there are fewer of the species although there are concentrations of the eagle in Etosha National Park in the Tsumkwe District and on central Namibian farmland. There is very little information available about how many breeding pairs there actually are or how many make up the total population, however, estimates have indicated that there may be up to 600 breeding pairs in South Africa and around 350 pairs across Namibia.

The eagle inhabits a wide range of environments and favours open grassland and savannah – where large trees may grow – and wooded savannah, although they do not like dense forests. Where trees are sparse, the eagle is known to inhabit pylons. Closed-canopy forests and extremely arid deserts do not make a good environment for this fierce predator, but it does live near rivers (where trees are enormous). The eagle feeds on up to 403 different species and, out of these, around 65% of its diet is made up of mongooses (including meerkats) and hares. It is also a scavenger and likes to feed on carrion or small livestock that has been left rotting in the open. In northeast South Africa

it feeds mainly on birds, particularly game birds, but small mammals are still a prerequisite. Not a great deal of information is available on the bird's diet in Namibia but it is known to prey on meerkats.

Adults are generally solitary birds and stay close to their nests all year round. Martial eagles breed during the winter months (particularly in Namibia) and usually one egg is produced. In a study carried out in the early 1990s, three pairs were followed over the course of three years and it was discovered that one egg was laid in alternate years. For a species that is endangered, this is a low number of offspring and is certainly not considered a positive discovery with regard to ensuring that the species survives long term. In a study of one pair over a further 13 years, just six eggs were hatched and only three young reached independence.

Threats facing Martial eagles include being shot or drowned (in farmland reservoirs), and the population is estimated to have reduced dramatically, by around 80% in just five years. Some birds suffer from poisoning and others find their days numbered when they collide with power lines. There are also concerns that declining numbers are due to a reduction in available prey, which severely limits the eagle's population. The eagle is not, however, classed worldwide as endangered. In South Africa the Martial eagle is classed as 'vulnerable' where a decline of 20% in the population has caused some concern. With a wingspan of easily six feet, the Martial eagle makes an easy meal of an adult meerkat while smaller birds of prey are known to prey on the pups.

Despite the threat these large eagles are to meerkats and other small mammals, today farmers are educated in the preservation of these birds. Although the eagle is thought to attack some domestic stock, it has been shown that this is more likely to be as a result of scavenging and that this element of the Martial eagle's diet is only a small fraction of its total consumption. Farmers are actively encouraged to protect nests and many farm reservoirs are now covered to prevent drowning in arid areas. Meerkats signal effectively to warn the mob of an impending attack from the sky. They all sprint for bolt-holes, but if none are nearby then they will lie still on the ground and rely on camouflage for protection. Sometimes they will take refuge in thorny bushes where eagles will not dare to land.

Jackals

When meerkats are not facing a swooping threat from the skies they are on the lookout for those predators on four legs that are quick, agile and fairly intelligent. The jackal is one such hunter of meerkats. These highly adaptable and intelligent animals are not in fact the 'dirty scavengers' they have long been labelled as. There are at least three, if not four, species of jackal and their characteristics rarely overlap. The most common features between the three main types are their size and ears. The Golden Jackal (Canis aureas) is the most common, while the Black-backed Jackal (Canis mesomelas) is the next most

prevalent. The third species is the Side-striped Jackal (Canis adustus), which is sadly endangered, followed by the Simien Jackal (Canis simians), which is often described as a fox or wolf and believed to be more closely related to wolves than jackals. The Black-backed Jackal and the Side-striped Jackal are the two species thought to have evolved in Africa.

Their typical diet consists of insects, small rodents and fruit, but couples or groups will co-operate to attack gazelles and impalas. They will feed on carrion should a decaying animal be lying on the savannah, but otherwise they are not scavengers. If brave enough, the jackal will also take a piece of meat from under a larger predator's nose, such as kill from a lion. Even though they are smaller and weigh around a third less than a hyena, the jackal will take kill from this larger prey if they are hungry. So, in reality, the jackal is quite brave. Another admirable attribute is, like meerkats, their loyalty and solidarity with family members.

Most jackals will mate for life, although some are more flippant about the nature

of life with one partner. They are, however, extremely loyal and Black-backed Jackals in particular – once part of a pair – do everything together from playing to hunting. Another thing that jackals share with meerkats is having 'helpers',

whereby pups that reach adulthood and have not yet left the family help to rear the next litter, which increases the chances of the babies' survival and goes some way to ensuring greater numbers in the population.

Originally from Persia, the jackal is currently found in Africa, southeast Europe and Asia. In Africa, the jackal fills an ecological niche in much the same way the coyote does in North America as a lesser predator. With their long legs and curved, canine teeth, the jackal is adept at hunting small mammals, birds and reptiles. Their blunt feet and fused leg bones give them the perfect frame for running long distances and they are capable of maintaining speeds of around 10 mph (16 km/h). Unfortunately for meerkats, jackals are most active early in the morning or at dusk. Like meerkats, jackals mark their territories and defend them fiercely with scent markings, including urine and faeces.

Although they occasionally assemble in small groups for hunting they are more likely to hunt alone or in pairs. Despite this mammal's predatory powers, however, a mob of meerkats does have the ability to chase off a jackal if they all stick together.

Cobras

Cobras are another cause of concern for the mob. These venomous snakes are renowned for their deadly bite. It is not unusual for the mob to try to intimidate a cobra during daylight hours to make sure that it does not try to 'steal' into the burrow by following the meerkats.

Found in Africa as well as south Asia and the Philippines, cobras are easily recognised by the hoods that flare behind their heads when they are angry or threatened. Most cobras average around 12 feet and are often thin and coloured olive or brown. Northern South Africa is renowned for the spitting, or black-necked cobra that can spray its venom from a distance of eight feet quite accurately. The rinkhals, or ringhals, is a different type of spitting cobra and is found in South Africa where it averages around four feet in length. This snake is generally dark brown or black with ridged scales and light rings on its neck. The most common cobra in the Kalahari is the asp or Egyptian cobra, which

will seldom attack unless provoked. Meerkats, however, don't want to take any chances. If threatened, though, the cobra will strike.

There are many different species of cobra while the King Cobra is the only one that will make a nest (on the ground) in which to hatch its young. These snakes will lay around 20 to 40 eggs, which is heavily guarded by the female and her mate. Hatchlings, which take around 70-90 days to incubate, are around 20 inches long. King Cobras are the longest venomous snakes in the world and have an amazing sense of smell. They are a threat to meerkat pups, but the meerkats themselves and other members of the mongoose family who are immune to their venom also prey them on. Meerkats are renowned for mobbing a cobra if it strays too close to the burrow and their agile abilities ensure that most times they avoid the venom of this reptile. They have also been known to kill a cobra if the threat was deemed too great. Puff header snakes also like to prey on meerkat pups but the 'mobbing' by the gang that precedes any would-be attack is often too much of a threat for the snake, and the reptile is more likely to move on than risk a repeat attack for the sake of a meal.

CHAPTER 6

A **DAY IN THE LIFE** OF A **MEERKAT**

The Weather and Other Meekats

It is, indeed, not just the African wildlife that threatens meerkats; the weather can be a danger too. Meerkats are renowned for disliking the rain. If it is raining they will remain in the burrow until the wet weather has passed. Even foraging for food will be put on hold, which (when it is considered that meerkats eat little and often) cannot be easy when there is a huge and prolonged downpour.

Summer rains are a particular threat and when precipitation approaches the sentry will sound the alarm. Newborn pups need to be on higher ground at this time as they will drown if the burrow is flooded. The alpha female takes the young, one by one, to higher ground to avoid this risk.

Another threat comes from rival mobs or gangs. If another gang has happened to encroach on the mob's territory then the alarm signal from the sentry will sound. Fights are fierce and often lead to fatalities, as submission is the primary goal. The larger group is often the winner and then the burrow in question is usually taken over. Unfortunately for some mob members, meerkats rely on smell and if a family member happens to have been in combat and smell of a rival then they are often attacked by their own.

After a conflict, mob members will hug and congratulate each other and then re-mark each other from the saliva or anal gland. Because of the confusion that often follows a fight, non-dominant meerkats will often join the rival group and reclaim the burrow on the winning side. One of the reasons for this may well be down to smell, as the winning side may welcome the meerkat because its smell is familiar, while the meerkat's own losing side may well want to fight because the smell is that of a rival.

Once the meerkat (usually the one that has been the last into the burrow the night before) has emerged and established that the environment is once again safe for all, the meerkats dart around on the highest point of the sand or dirt mounds outside the burrow, while others reaffirm their bonds by grooming each other.

One of the most usual activities at the start of the day is for meerkats to warm their abdomens as the sun wends its way higher into the sky. As a small mammal, it is difficult for a meerkat to regulate its temperature sufficiently and the cold is something that it easily suffers from. The alpha male – sometimes the female – will give a call signal after about an hour or so, which leads the

meerkats in a particular direction.

Despite the fast movement of the mob, many stop to dig or forage for insects and other food sources along the way. Their tails, high in the air, help them to distinguish where their family members are. Just as often as they dig, meerkats will stand erect looking out for danger or other members of the mob. Most foraging adults will eat first and then feed young pups that are learning the ropes about foraging for food. Pups are renowned for their loud cries for food and although they remain close to their mentor, any member of the group may feed a pup that is crying out to be fed. When the sun is high and the temperature is soaring it is usual for the group to rest.

It is at the end of the day when researchers have commented on how meerkats' individual personalities are most distinguishable. Some meerkats have had enough and just want to burrow down for the night. Others, however, want to play and socialise. Some are only interested in finding that last bit of food that will see them through until morning. As the sun begins to set meerkats will take in the last rays to help keep them warm before night falls.

CHAPTER 7

THE **MEERKAT MANOR** PHENOMENON

The concept for Meerkat Manor came as a result of an extensive research project by academics at the University of Cambridge. It began in 1993 when Professor Tim Clutton-Brock from the University believed that meerkats could offer a vital insight into the evolution of mammalian co-operation. Cameras were put in place and tracking devices placed round certain meerkats' necks to record their movements, habitat, and interaction with other families of the same species.

The idea to create a long-running series came in 2004, and was the brainchild of executive producer at Oxford Scientific Films, Caroline Hawkins. Having been asked to present an idea for a new series for Animal Planet International, Caroline, knowing just how charismatic

PROFESSOR TIM CLUTTON-BROCK

the little furry creatures are, had a feeling that the concept would be a big hit. It was also at this time that meerkats were popping up all over the place – in advertising and marketing campaigns, on mugs, tea towels and coasters for gifts. The timing, in fact, couldn't have been better.

The filming manages to portray the best and the worst of meerkat society, which

captured on camera is cleverly turned into a stunning programme that portrays courage, violence and bonding, whilst managing to bring an exciting storyline to the viewer. What is unique, however, is how they managed to create an animal 'soap opera' out of the series, instead of the traditional format of a nature programme, documentary style.

Commissioned for Animal Planet by executive producer and commissioning editor Mark Wild, the inspiration for the series came from one of Caroline's previous films, The Wild Ladies of Viramba. Made for the BBC's Natural World series, they followed and filmed a wild troop of yellow baboons in Tanzania's Mikumi National Park. They did this with a difference, and that difference was applied to the concept of Meerkat Manor. Caroline describes how 'each of the baboons had been given a name by the researchers who were studying them and we came to know each as an individual character. It was just a natural transition for me then to transfer the strengths of that storytelling approach to Meerkat Manor. It also occurred to me that it would be fun to have several plots running

simultaneously in each show – just like a soap. Then we designed titles to be a bit like Dallas … and the title music to be a bit like Desperate Housewives … and the rest is history'.

Full of passion, intrigue, love, squabbling and self-sacrifice, this series was originally shown on Animal Planet via Sky, and on the BBC to audiences in the United States and the United Kingdom alike, and had as many viewers on the edge of their seats as BBC's EastEnders or ITV's Coronation Street. With storylines as complex and as exciting as 'human' soaps, Meerkat Manor was so successful in the U.K. and the U.S. that it soon aired on the national channels in Australia and Canada as well. The series has since been broadcast in over 160 countries worldwide, such has been its popularity.

Four series of Meerkat Manor were made between 2005 and 2008 and it has won numerous awards over the years. As well as being Animal Planet's top series in 2007, with audience ratings of over four million in the U.S. alone, it was also nominated for two Primetime Emmy Awards that year. It won three awards at the 2006 Onmi Awards, followed by a further two in that year and 2007 at the New York Festivals Award Galas. In 2008 the eighth episode of series three, 'Journey's End' won the Five Award for Best Popular Programme at the Wildscreen Festival Panada Awards. This particular episode depicted the death of Flower, the Whiskers matriarch, and prior to her death, the leading lady meerkat of Meerkat Manor.

The location for the series was at the Kuruman River Reserve in Northern Cape, South Africa, which is where the joint Cambridge University and the Kalahari Research Trust long term Kalahari Meerkat Project has been running.

The filming of each Meerkat Manor series took seven to eight months due to the fact that the film crew were limited to capturing the footage in the Kalahari spring and summer seasons only, as during the winter months meerkats are a lot less active.

The overall structure of the series primarily followed the meerkat mob called the Whiskers. Originally a group of 29 meerkats, this group was chosen for the series because of their particularly dominant matriarch already mentioned, Flower. Unusually in the meerkat world, Flower remained the dominant female and led the group for five years until her death as a result of a snake bite during series three. Her daughter Rocket Dog took over from where her mother had left off. Other meerkat mobs as rivals and neighbours, also named by the film crew, play an intrinsic part in the series as a whole and include the Lazuli mob, the Commandos, the Zappa mob and the Starsky mob. The interaction of the Whiskers mob over a long period of time with these other gangs of meerkats shows just how dangerous, sometimes fickle and cruel the world in which they live is.

Also integral to the overall style and impact of Meerkat Manor was some of the equipment and technique used for filming the footage. Although the Sony DSR570 cameras were used for the majority of the series, other innovative methods were employed. The use of mini fibre-optic infra-red cameras were used to capture footage inside the meerkats' burrows, and wireless microphones were used to capture and

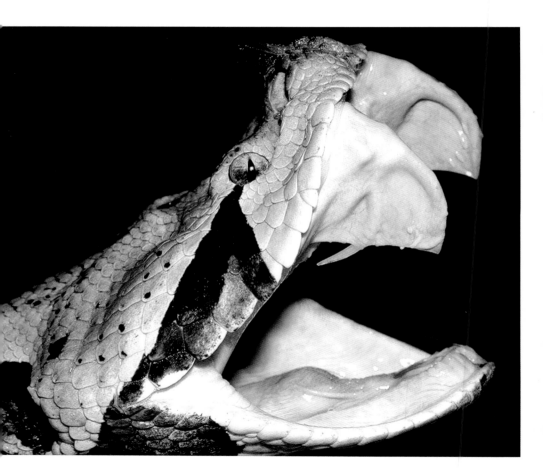

record the numerous noises meerkats make for specific (and often life saving) purposes. Radio collars were also fitted, usually to the dominant female of each group filmed, so that the mobs could be tracked. These innovative new methods have given the scientists working on the Kalahari Project the opportunity for the first time to study aspects of meerkats' lives that, until the filming of Meerkat Manor, had never been seen before.

The Meerkat Manor series at all times upholds the research group's policy of not interfering with the natural lives and deaths of the meerkats. This, however, has been one of the main criticisms that the series has had from fans, particularly following the death of Flower. Why are snake-bitten meerkats not injected with anti-venom to save them? Why are injured meerkats allowed to suffer in front of the camera and then die when they could have been put out of their misery? Well, executive producer Mick Kaczorowski from the United States has commented on this criticism with the facts: the film crew and researchers 'don't want to have an effect on the gene pool by saving a weaker meerkat [or] affecting the outcome of what's natural in the Kalahari'. The whole purpose of

the research project is to capture and study the natural process of breeding and survival, and what factors in the lives of meerkats affect this. If, in fact, human intervention occurred it would render years and years of research results useless. The only exception to this rule during the filming of Meerkat Manor was with regard to any outbreaks of tuberculosis. In these instances the meerkats would be euthanised in order to prevent an outbreak of the disease, which would seriously threaten both cattle in the region and the meerkat population as a whole.

Perhaps the only arguably negative aspect of this new soap-like style production meant that audiences become very emotionally involved with the meerkats, unlike the effect that a traditional nature documentary has on its audience, which is much more matter of fact and retains an emotional distance from their subjects. James Poniewozik of Time Magazine commented on this aspect of the series in a 2007 article stating that, 'Like the meerkats, Manor is an odd beast. The crew is forbidden to intervene, and the producers don't sugarcoat the animals' less cuddly habits (infidelity, abandonment of young, occasional cannibalism). But the meerkats are named and given human traits ('courageous,' 'caring,' 'bully[ing]'), and their antics and tragedies take place over a sound track. Manor is both brutal and melodramatic and thus more devastating than most documentary or scripted drama.'

The first series of Meerkat Manor introduces the Whiskers mob to the viewers for the first time. The basics of everyday

WHISKERS MOB

meerkat life, including the importance of foraging, predators, grooming, being a sentry, being a babysitter and the role of the dominant female (in this case Flower) with regard to hierarchy and breeding is all covered in the first series.

As events in the Whiskers mob unfolds other meerkat mobs are introduced to the series, and there are family feuds, evictions, deaths and much more.

Once the audience had been educated about the basics of everyday meerkat life, the following episodes focused on using the dramas and exciting events caught on camera for the bulk of the series' material. This was undoubtedly a production decision that had an enormous influence on the series becoming 'soap-opera' like in style as opposed to the style of a traditional nature documentary.

As the different meerkat mobs get on with their lives, the mating, rivalries, fighting, family feuding, evictions, killings of each other and deaths caused by predators all amalgamate into a highly complex and fluid social system. Meerkats that are born into one particular mob don't necessarily stay with that mob for the rest of their lives. They can be evicted by their own and join a rival gang, or they may leave their gang of their own accord (especially if there has been a battle for the dominant position in the group) and start a new one.

Meerkats, therefore, who were in certain families at the beginning of the filming of Meerkat Manor, would not necessarily still be there by the end of the final series.

Naturally, it is impossible to document the detail of every single

WHISKERS MOB

meerkat's life, movements and exploits here. Watching the Meerkat Manor series from start to finish is the only way to really grasp the bigger picture and get a totally rounded appreciation of these fascinating and charismatic little furry creatures. However, a basic introduction to the various main players and different rival meerkat mobs involved

in the series is certainly possible.

With the territory of at least two square miles in the Kuruman River Reserve, the Whiskers mob was first identified as a unified group in 1998. For the purpose of this particular mob (who form the core characters of Meerkat Manor) the introduction to the Whiskers gang shall start in 2002 when Flower became the matriarch following the death of her predecessor, Vialli.

In the first series Zaphod is introduced as the dominant male and Flower's faithful mate, this was not always the case, however. With Flower in the driving seat Yossarian (Zaphod's younger brother) overthrew Zaphod for a time, albeit Zaphod fighting back and regain-

FLOWER

ing his position, which is where he was at the beginning of Meerkat Manor.

Flower's dominance resulted in the new meerkat mob called Starsky being formed following the eviction of her daughters Kinkaju, Mozart and two other female meerkats. Much to the distress of all Meerkat Manor fans who had been glued to the series from day one, Flower was bitten by a snake in January 2007 and died as a result; this was during series three. Rocket Dog, her daughter took over as the dominant female following a battle with her sister

ROCKET DOG

Maybelline. Zaphod was also not happy with Rocket Dog being in charge and the situation caused the Whiskers mob to split in half, with some of the others forming the Aztecs.

Flower was such a focal point of Meerkat Manor for so long, and it affected so many fans when she died that it is only right and a tribute to her, if you like, to look at her life in more detail here. In fact, viewers all over the world had become so attached to her through watching the series that, as well as the backlash about her being allowed to die, she was mourned as if she were a much-loved human celebrity.

In the United States, United Press International released an obituary-like news story following the announcement of her demise. The demand for Flower having a proper memorial page was so great that the Animal Planet website in the States added a special page as a memorial to her. Fans also put video tributes on YouTube, as well as writing letters and poems.

Had the world gone mad I hear you cry? Perhaps! Or maybe this reaction is

ROCKET DOG

became the matriarch of the Whiskers mob two years later and was the mother to an estimated 70 pups over her lifetime. Following the birth of pups by her daughters, Tosca and Mozart, Flower accepted them for the first seven weeks of their lives, which she didn't have to do. She could have killed them or evicted her daughters immediately. Both daughters did, however, get evicted permanently in the end.

Described as a tough, strong leader who ruled with an 'iron paw', Flower also had a soft and endearing side. As

just a huge compliment to the Meerkat Manor film crew and production team; how many other nature documentaries ever made could have touched the lives of so many that this kind of reaction is generated? The only other similar scenario that comes to mind is when the Coronation Street character Deirdre Rachid was sent to prison and the storyline led to a campaign to free her being printed in the tabloid newspapers, as well as Downing Street receiving a petition, which led to Tony Blair calling for her release. Utterly ludicrous? It still happened!

So, the bottom line is that Flower was a meerkat celebrity – the Princess Diana of Meerkat Manor. She was born on 15th March 2000 and, as mentioned,

FLOWER'S PUPS

a devoted mother she was extremely gentle with the pups (even when they were not her own), and she showed great affection to her entire Whiskers

family. Her heroism was displayed when she risked life and limb to find her lost pups that had strayed into rival mob Zappa territory, and she also took in an abandoned pup called Axel from that very group. It would have been quite normal behaviour for a matriar-

AXEL

chal meerkat to kill such an intruder. It was in fact Flower's natural protective and powerful instincts as a mother that led to her death. Faced with a deadly predator, the Cape Cobra snake, Flower took a bite in the face whilst trying to protect a newly born litter of pups from the snake.

The 2008 Animal Planet film, Meerkat Manor: The Story Begins, is in fact a film biography of Flower's early life and rise to the top of the Whiskers mob.

Other main members of the Whiskers mob (well, they were part of it at the start of Meerkat Manor in any case), and a few already mentioned above, include Yossarian, Shakespeare, Tosca, Daisy, Mitch, Rocket Dog, Axel and Sophie.

Named after the main character in Catch-22, Yossarian was Zaphod's younger brother and, prior to Meerkat Manor, Flower's mate. He had also been the dominant male before Flower became the matriarch, with her sister in fact. In the opening credits of the series Yossarian is described as the meerkat with 'social problems' then later as 'troubled'. Poor Yossarian didn't seem to be able to get much right.

Even when the idea was potentially a good one, like moving burrows for example, he always seemed to mess everything up and create havoc, not to mention putting his fellow gang and their pups in grave danger. He was ostracised on one particular occasion when his actions resulted in the death of a newborn pup. He did, however, get

SHAKESPEARE

some things right and when he did he saved the lives of pups. Yossarian ended up leaving the group towards the end of the second series and became a roving meerkat for good it seems, as he was never seen on camera again.

Poor Shakespeare, one of Flower's sons, played an intrinsic part of the storyline but he was only present until the end of the first series. Described as 'courageous' in the opening credits, Shakespeare first survived a bite by a puff adder snake and then got honourably stuck into his daily chores with his fellow gang members.

Babysitting and therefore protecting Whiskers pups at the time of a Lazuli attack, however, Shakespeare was last seen by the camera crew in between them and Big Si from the aforementioned mob. Shakespeare was never caught on film again, so no one really knows what happened to him. Thomas Flower from the Kalahari Meerkat Project commented on the situation with Shakespeare as follows: '... meerkats are often killed defending pups, Shakespeare was a babysitter the day before and Lazuli were in the area. However, it is equally possible that he was killed by a predator, dispersed to another group, or was killed by another group whilst trying to join them, we just weren't there on that particular day'.

'Rebellious' Tosca, as described in the opening credits of the first series, was one of Flower's eldest daughters and, like Shakespeare, only starred in the

MITCH

CARLOS

moving burrows with the rest of the Whiskers. She chose the family and had to leave her pups to die.

A rare and unfortunate event happened to Daisy when her sister Mozart evicted her from the Whiskers. Mozart got her comeuppance in the end, however, and eventually got permanently evicted by Flower herself, whilst Daisy was allowed to rejoin the mob.

In the long run Daisy proved to be a great asset to the Whiskers and on two separate occasions fought off and protected the pups from rival mob attacks. By the time Daisy became pregnant by a roving Zappa male, Rocket Dog was the matriarch and luckily for her did not evict her. At the time of filming the very last episode for the series, she had just given birth to the litter.

Appearing in the very first episode of Meerkat Manor, 'heroic' Mitch, as he became known, was only three weeks old and nearly didn't make it to the end of the very first episode after his older siblings abandoned him in the desert! He then miraculously averted death a second time after he ate a poisonous

first series. She came to blows with her mother too many times and, despite her efforts to rejoin the Whiskers on several occasions, failed. Flower wouldn't allow it. Before she disappeared for good, presumed to have succumbed to the harsh winter in between filming, she did mate with the roving meerkat Carlos. Perhaps if he had shown more long-term interest in her they would have started a new gang together, but he didn't and she wasn't seen again.

Strangely enough, the roving ex-Lazuli male Carlos, had the nickname of Casanova, and one of Flower's other daughters, Daisy, was one of the first to be wooed by him. Traumatic times followed and led to Daisy having to choose between her newborn pups and insect that he had stolen from one of the adult meerkats.

Mitch made it through his early years somehow, and during the second and third series he was fast growing into a responsible adult. He was frequently trying to save the day, which usually meant pups. Sometimes he was successful and other times tragically not, but, akin to the late Shakespeare, his heart was always in the right place. He was the one who saved the abandoned Zappa pup called Axel and took him back to the Whiskers. It was a rare event in meerkat society when Axel was accepted and adopted by them. Normally an abandoned rival pup would have been killed instantly.

By the end of the fourth series, Mitch was doing just fine, still massively contributing to the Whiskers community and looking more than likely to move to the dominant male position at any time. Axel had adjusted to his new family life, albeit following Mitch around most of the time!

The new Whiskers matriarch, following the devastating death of her mother,

Rocket Dog appeared to find it slightly daunting being in charge of such a large mob at first. She had had some previous experience, however. Earlier on the group had temporarily split in the third series because of drought and lack of sustenance, and she assumed leadership of that splinter group. Her eventual takeover from Flower caused some controversy within the Whiskers, which in fact created long-term family changes.

Zaphod stood by her side for a while fending off unwanted advances from rival and roving males, but he eventually left the gang for good to rove himself, and eventually became the dominant male of the Aztecs. Her sister Maybelline also failed to usurp her from dominance and she also left for good, and in fact started the new mob of Aztecs. Having survived a deadly puff adder bite, tragically it appeared that Rocket Dog was killed after the final episode of the fourth series had been filmed, but before the first episode of Meerkat Manor was broadcast.

One of Mozart's pups, Sophie didn't feature a huge amount earlier on in

the series, but was seen much more in the fourth, 'The Next Generation'. If anything, Sophie was predominantly known for two things: being an excellent babysitter and for being a hot target for roving male meerkats! Rocket Dog had evicted her for mating with Wilson, who had already mated with Rocket Dog, but allowed her to rejoin the group once she aborted the litter. Sophie somehow managed to get evicted again (by another female meerkat, Wiley Kat), and even though she became pregnant again, managed to rejoin her old gang, and this time gave birth successfully to three pups. Following Rocket Dog's death, Sophie became the new and current Whiskers dominant female.

The Lazuli - the Whiskers' archenemies

One of the oldest and most successful meerkat groups that live within the area of the Kalahari Meerkat Project, the Lazuli group was originally formed in 1995. The gang was named after

THE LAZULI

their very first dominant female Lazuli and has since grown to be one of the largest, and includes meerkats that have become well known to the researchers over the numerous years of study.

By the time the film crews of Meerkat Manor came along, Cazanna was the group's long-term dominant female. Her dominant male partner, Big Si, died between the filming of the first and second series and her son Carlos took over the role, leaving Cazanna without a mating partner. Before the death of Big Si from tuberculosis, the film crew had labelled him as 'the biggest, meanest meerkat in the territory'.

CAZANNA

As the dominant Lazuli male he was responsible for masterminding regular attacks on the Whiskers' burrow. It is also thought (although not known for sure) that he could have been responsible for the death of Whiskers meerkat Shakespeare.

THE COMMANDOS

Despite the efforts of various Whiskers meerkats, including Yossarian, none of them managed to break through the male defence of the Lazuli group to mate with Cazanna. Yossarian eventually mated with Cazanna's daughter Pancake, however, and although she was evicted from the gang, Cazanna took her back in. In between the filming of series three and four, Cazanna died, which left Pancake as the dominant female of the group.

The Commandos

The Commandos appear as a new enemy gang to the Whiskers early on in the second series and they have regular confrontations with them. At one point there is a conflict involving the three meerkat mobs – Whiskers, Lazuli and Commandos.

Hannibal, an aggressive, one-eyed meerkat with his remaining eye firmly looking at dominance and victory, led the Commandos until his death during the winter before the beginning of the fourth series. Rivalling Zaphod in terms of physical size, he was one of the Kalahari's largest meerkats and has been described as a 'just a plain mean bully no one wants to see'. Hannibal was no stranger to leading a confrontation and he headed up many attacks against the Whiskers, Lazuli and Zappa mobs during his reign. He ruled the mob with his partner, the dominant Commandos female Nikita. His son Wilson was second in command before he became a roving male throughout the third and fourth series.

A good match for Hannibal, Nikita was also a meerkat not to be messed with and was intrinsic in many raids on rival burrows, including being a part of the killing of a Lazuli pup, and she actually led the attack and murder of Whiskers-evicted Mozart's newborn pups. She also had no qualms in evicting 80% of the Commandos females from the mob when she was pregnant herself in the final series. Most of the females evicted were in fact her daughters.

Following the death of Hannibal, Nikita had one litter of pups by ex-Whiskers, now roving male Seacrest, but eventually choose another ex-Whiskers rover Zorro as her permanent partner. In an unusual display of compassion she also allowed four of his brothers to join the Commandos.

Zorro's dominant behaviour created new controversies, when, what is thought to be the first time ever, he evicted his own brother Miles for getting too close to Nikita. Never previously on Meerkat Manor had a male been sent into exile. Unfortunately Zorro didn't make it to the end of the fourth series and, given the fact that his radio collar was found hanging from a tree, the presumption was that he had been killed by a bird of prey.

The Zappa mob

It is perhaps no surprise with regard to this mob's title that they were named after the musician Frank Zappa. Although the group came into existence in 2001 they didn't actually feature in Meerkat Manor until the third series, by which time they had moved in beside the Whiskers, becoming their new neighbours. The Whiskers first encounter the rival Zappa mob at the beginning of the third series when Flower strayed into their territory on the hunt for better foraging grounds. On the DVD title credits the Zappa mob are subtitled, 'the neighbours from hell', need any more be said? Throughout the third series the two have altercations on numerous occasions, often caused by turf wars as one or the other tried to take or regain some territory.

When the Zappa mob first became an integral part of Meerkat Manor the group consisted of 14 meerkats. The dominant female was Lola and the dominant male Frank. By the middle of the third series, however, the leadership roles of both male and female meerkats changed. Lola had suffered an injury from a puff adder snake. In a weakened state during her recovery her sister Punk seized the opportunity and took over as the gang's new matriarch. Lola did in fact accept her sister as the new leader, even after she had recovered from her snakebite.

The male Zappa fraternity decided to make some changes in parallel with the female hierarchy shift. Frank, who had been another fearless and formidable leader, was in fact usurped and forced into exile by his younger brother

THE ZAPPA MOB

Houdini. The film crew did not in fact see Frank again after this event. Houdini was regarded somewhat as the second Casanova of the Kalahari (after Carlos had quietened down that is) and managed to mate with Flower when she was alive, plus her daughter Maybelline. His new role as head male Zappa meant that his attention turned to protecting the females in his own mob from such advances from the likes of the mobless and roving Zaphod and Wilson.

LOLA

Punk accepted Houdini as her new partner and the Zappa mob continued to live dangerously, flitting in and out of Whiskers territory on foraging runs. Due to the fact that the Zappa mob were much smaller in number compared with the Whiskers, they often sensibly took the flight instead of fight option if faced with a potential confrontation.

The Starsky mob

The Starsky mob was formed in between the filming of the second and third Meerkat Manor series. The group only consisted of seven meerkats with Mozart and Carlos, who formed it, as the dominant female and male partners respectively. Mozart and Kinkajou (the sisters who were evicted from the Whiskers) did compete for matriarchal position but Mozart won the crown, for a while. Kinkajou, however, having also mated with Carlos, quickly asserted her dominance over Mozart by killing her newborn pups, taking the lead on foraging trips and commanding a move to a new burrow.

Carlos, having been evicted from the Lazuli mob had been a roving meerkat for a while, so this was the perfect opportunity to establish himself as head of a new mob. Unfortunately, the new gang was not destined to last long and it sadly turned out to be the beginning of the end for many of them.

During a fight with the formidable Commandos' Hannibal, Carlos received a vicious bite on his face and he eventually died of his injuries. This left the females without a dominant male. As well as sisters Mozart and Kinkajou, there was also their third-evicted Whiskers sister, De la Soul.

Towards the end of the third series, the Starsky mob, in fact, only consisted of the three sisters. Hard enough for the three female meerkats to cope on their own, they were struggling to survive. What they didn't need was a run-in with the Commandos. They were forced to flee for their lives and in the process De la Soul got separated from her sisters. She was never seen again and presumed dead. Mozart and Kinkajou managed to escape to a burrow and took shelter there from a night-time storm. It was there that Kinkajou died in her sleep, most probably from being too weak.

Mozart was now totally alone, and meerkats don't tend to survive very long when they are alone. Help seemed to be

at hand, however, and there was a glimmer of hope when she met the roving Commandos male, Wilson. Tragically, just when it looked as if the pair could create a new gang, a jackal just outside the burrow killed Mozart.

THE STARSKY MOB

Mozart was a very popular meerkat to the audience of Meerkat Manor, and she was killed just under a month after her mother Flower was. The public reaction to the news, again reported in the national newspapers, was similar to when the news of Flower's death was reported. Tributes were uploaded by Mozart fans including songs, poems and videos.

The Aztecs

When Rocket Dog became the dominant female of the Whiskers (following the death of her mother Flower), by the end of the third series her sister Maybelline had broken away from them and formed the Aztecs.

MAYBELLINE FORMES THE AZTECS

They were another small group of meerkats with only seven adults in the gang when they first formed. Throughout the fourth series they became part of the Whiskers' rivalry furniture. Ex-Whisker and until then rover, Zaphod, not only joined the Aztecs, but brought a gang of other roving males with him. Zaphod naturally took up his position as dominant male. Unfortunately Maybelline was his daughter, so he didn't have a mate. Zaphod, the wise grandfather of Meerkat Manor and named after Zaphod Beeblebrox from The Hitchhiker's Guide to the Galaxy, died naturally of old age; he was 12. This of course left the Aztecs without a dominant male at the end of the fourth and final series.

The Research Project Continues

Since the end of Meerkat Manor in 2008 the Kalahari Meerkat Project continues its research into the lives of meerkats and is now part of Cambridge University's 'Large Animal Research Group'. The project is still headed up by Professor Tim Clutton-Brock, FRS. A dozen or so volunteers who are supervised by Helene Brettschneider (Field Coordinator) and James Samson, (Field Manager) help the project, which covers an area of approximately 20 square miles of the Kalahari Desert. In addition to Professor Tim Clutton-Brock (Professor of Animal Ecology), the other principal on the project is Professor Marta Manser, Professor of Animal Behaviour at the University of Zurich.

The Kalahari Meerkat Project is actually focused on studying 16 different groups of meerkats. As the research continues the focus remains to collate data so that an extremely accurate picture can be built up with regard to the meerkats' complete life history, including all changes in groups, social status, births, deaths, mating patterns and cycles, as well as all 'out of character' or abnormal activities and behaviour.

The meerkats have become accustomed to the presence of the researchers and film crews. This situation also provides a platform for other wildlife researchers, and the project team has hosted a number of other film crews for different productions. Apart from Meerkat

DAVID ATTENBOROUGH

Manor, the BBC has filmed a meerkat episode for Sir David Attenborough's series Life of Mammals, a National Geographic special called Walking with Meerkats: Meerkat Madness has been filmed, as well as the 2003 Nigel Marven film Meerkats.

Founded in Switzerland in 2007, the 'Friends of the Kalahari Meerkat Project' was set up to fund the on-going research project. The organisation's website (http://friends.kalahari-meerkats.com) shows historical information about the project and also posts regular meerkat research updates with photos and video footage. To help raise money for the project a 'Friends' package can now also be bought, giving people access to additional information not included free on the website. There is also an e-store where meerkat merchandise can be purchased from shoes to mouse mats. All funds raised go towards the research project.

Design & Artwork: ALEX YOUNG

Published by: DEMAND MEDIA LIMITED & G2 ENTERTAINMENT LIMITED

Publishers: JASON FENWICK & JULES GAMMOND

Written by: MICHELLE BRACHET